Little Business Books

Resilience

Written by **Ruth Percival**
Illustrated by **Dean Gray**

Published in 2026 by Windmill Books,
an Imprint of Rosen Publishing
2544 Clinton St.
Buffalo, NY 14224

First published in Great Britain in 2024 by Hodder & Stoughton
Copyright © Hodder & Stoughton Limited, 2024

Credits
Series Editor: Amy Pimperton
Series Designer: Peter Scoulding
Consultant: Philippa Anderson
Philippa Anderson has a business degree and is a writer
and communications consultant who advises multinationals.
She authors and contributes to business books.

Cataloging-in-Publication Data

Names: Percival, Ruth, author. | Grey, Dean, illustrator.
Title: Resilience / Ruth Percival, illustrated by Dean Grey.
Description: Buffalo, NY : Windmill Books, 2026. | Series: Little business books | Includes glossary and index.
Identifiers: ISBN 9781725396524 (pbk.) | ISBN 9781725396531 (library bound) | ISBN 9781725396548 (ebook)
Subjects: LCSH: Resilience (Personality trait)--Juvenile literature. | Success in business--Juvenile literature.
Classification: LCC BF698.35.R47 P478 2026 | DDC 155.2'4--dc23

All rights reserved.

All facts and statistics were up to date at the time of press.

No part of this book may be reproduced in any form without permission
in writing from the publisher, except by a reviewer.

Printed in the United States of America

CPSIA Compliance Information: Batch #CSWM26
For Further Information contact Rosen Publishing at 1-800-237-9932

Find us on

Contents

4	What Is Resilience?
6	Stay Positive
8	Turn Problems Around
10	Admit When You're Wrong
12	Talk It Through
14	Don't Give Up
16	Ask for Help
18	Learn from Criticism
20	Learn from Mistakes
22	Don't Worry, Be Confident!
24	Plan for Problems
26	Work Hard
28	Believe in Yourself
30	Resilience and You
31	Notes for Sharing This Book
32	Glossary

What Is Resilience?

Resilience is how well you cope with and bounce back from challenges.

For example, moving to a new school can be scary at first, but in time you will be okay. Remember that no one is good at everything. Being happy that you tried your best shows that you have good resilience.

Sometimes, being resilient can feel hard. You might be afraid to try something new in case you fail. Sometimes, it can be difficult to know what to do when things go wrong.

WHY IS RESILIENCE IMPORTANT?

In business, resilience is important. Resilience can help a business to learn from problems, find out what customers want, and plan for the future.

For you, resilience might mean bouncing back from a mistake or asking for help when you need it.

What will our animal friends find out about resilience in business and about themselves?

Stay Positive

Pip Penguin feels sad. Her old business closed because it didn't make enough money.

Milly Monkey's support helps Pip to feel more positive.

Staying positive helps Pip Penguin think of a new business idea. Everyone loves ice-skating and Pip has the perfect place for a new ice rink!

Stay positive when things change.
This shows great resilience.

Turn Problems Around

The animals using Kit Kangaroo's café for the free internet don't buy food or drinks. There are no tables for paying customers!

Kit knows how to turn this problem around.

Kit Kangaroo turns the upstairs of her café into a work hub. The animals pay to use it.

Problems can be a good thing. Use your resilience to find ways to solve them.

Admit When You're Wrong

Leon Lion is cross. He hasn't sold any gas-powered cars this week. Where are his customers?

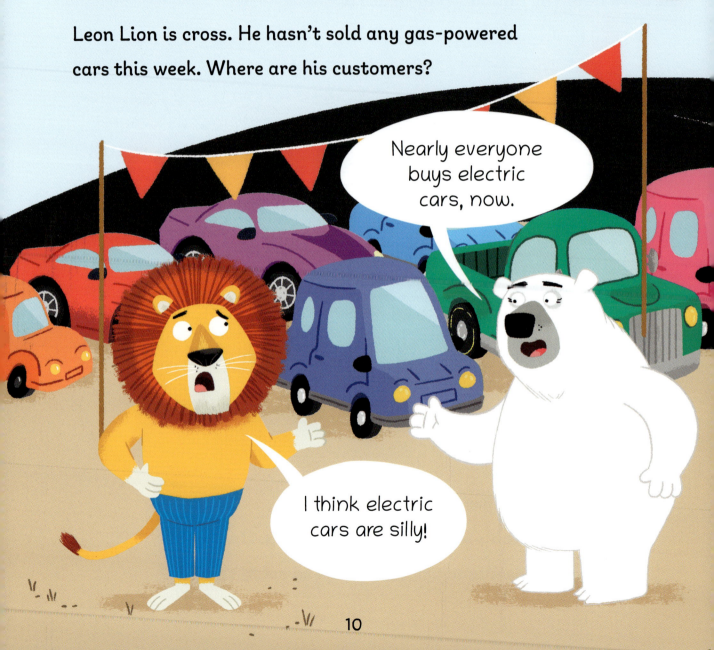

Then, Tilly Tiger zooms past, silently, in her awesome electric supercar.

Leon Lion realizes he is wrong. And Tilly's car has given him an idea ...

I'll sell electric cars, too!

If you get something wrong, it's brave to admit it!

Talk It Through

Big Business wants to order hundreds of Omar Owl's kites. But Big Business doesn't want to pay very much for them.

Soon, Omar Owl has good news ...

We agreed to a new deal that's fair to everyone!

If something isn't fair, talking things through can help you to stand up for yourself.

Don't Give Up

Last night, a huge storm blew down lots of trees at Kiki Koala's tree farm.

With Chip Cheetah's help, Kiki Koala plants new trees. She feels proud that she didn't give up.

Resilience can help you to bounce back and not give up.

Ask for Help

To get the job of making the big ice sculpture for the Snow Festival, Peggy Polar Bear must present her idea to the festival judges. Peggy feels scared!

Omar Owl helps Peggy Polar Bear practice her presentation. On the day, Peggy impresses the judges ... and gets the job!

If you feel afraid to do something, ask for help.

Learn from Criticism

Peter Panda puts spicy sauce on all the takeout pizzas he makes. But not all his customers like spicy pizza. Peggy Polar Bear complains!

Peter Panda doesn't like listening to criticism!

But when Peggy Polar Bear says she will never buy Peter's pizzas again, Peter listens – and saves his business.

Sorry, Peggy. Next time, I'll make your pizza not so spicy!

Criticism isn't always bad. It can help you to make better decisions.

Learn from Mistakes

Oops! Tilly Tiger has mixed up her customers' orders.

Tilly feels very silly. Will everyone think she's no good at running her business?

Milly Monkey gives Tilly Tiger some good advice.

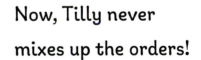

Slow down and check every order, twice.

Now, Tilly never mixes up the orders!

Everyone makes mistakes. Learning from them helps you build resilience.

Don't Worry, Be Confident!

Enzo Elephant sells toys and bikes. But Kiki Koala bought a new bike from Big Business instead.

It was so cheap!

Low prices make Big Business popular with customers. But Enzo isn't worried. He knows the toys and bikes he sells are better quality.

The next day, Kiki Koala's cheap bike breaks! Enzo Elephant is confident that Kiki will buy from him in the future.

When you feel confident, you worry less.

Plan for Problems

A herd of wildebeest has trampled Chip Cheetah's yoga studio. There's wildebeest poo everywhere! Chip can't run his yoga classes at the studio.

Work Hard

Wei Wolf wants his hat business to grow in the future.

Wei Wolf finds making T-shirts to be hard work at first, but he doesn't give up.

I'm so glad I kept going.

Wei's hard work has paid off. Now he has lots of T-shirts to sell to help his business grow.

Hard work takes resilience, but it's worth it.

Believe in Yourself

Milly Monkey has big plans for her treetop adventure park. She wants it to become a huge theme park, with rides and water slides! No one thinks Milly can do it.

But Milly Monkey believes in herself.
And she does it anyway.

When you are resilient, you believe in yourself.

Resilience and You

Our animal friends have learned a lot about resilience in business. What they have learned can help you to be resilient, too!

Tilly Tiger learned from a mistake. When you learn to not make the same mistakes again, your resilience grows.

Kit Kangaroo turned a problem into an opportunity. Resilience helps you to think positively when things go wrong.

Milly Monkey believed in herself. If you believe in yourself, then you are more likely to succeed.

Notes for Sharing This Book

This book introduces business ideas around the topic of resilience, which link to core personal and social resilience skills, such as persevering, asking for help, and self-confidence.

Talk about what business is and why we need good businesses. You can use each scenario to discuss themes of resilience. For example, you could talk about the child's feelings around a time they made a mistake or broke a favorite toy.

Resilience builds over time as we experience things and learn how to cope well with them. Resilience also needs an open and positive mind. For example, talk about a time when the child fell out with a friend. How did they feel? Were they able to talk through any problems and be friends again?

Glossary

advice a suggestion that can help you to make a decision or do something well

business a company that buys, makes, or sells goods or services to make money

criticism a comment about faults or mistakes

customer someone who buys things from a business

deal when two businesses agree to buy or supply goods or services for a certain price

electric car a car that is powered by electricity instead of fuel, such as gasoline

internet a computer network full of information and ways to communicate

supercar a type of sports car that can be driven on the road, rather than only on a race track

wildebeest a type of large African antelope

work hub a place where people pay money to use a desk and internet, instead of working at home or in an office